Amazing Creatures of the Arctic Ocean

Learn About Animals Including Polar Bears, Narwhals, Seals, and Sea Spiders!

Tamra B. Orr

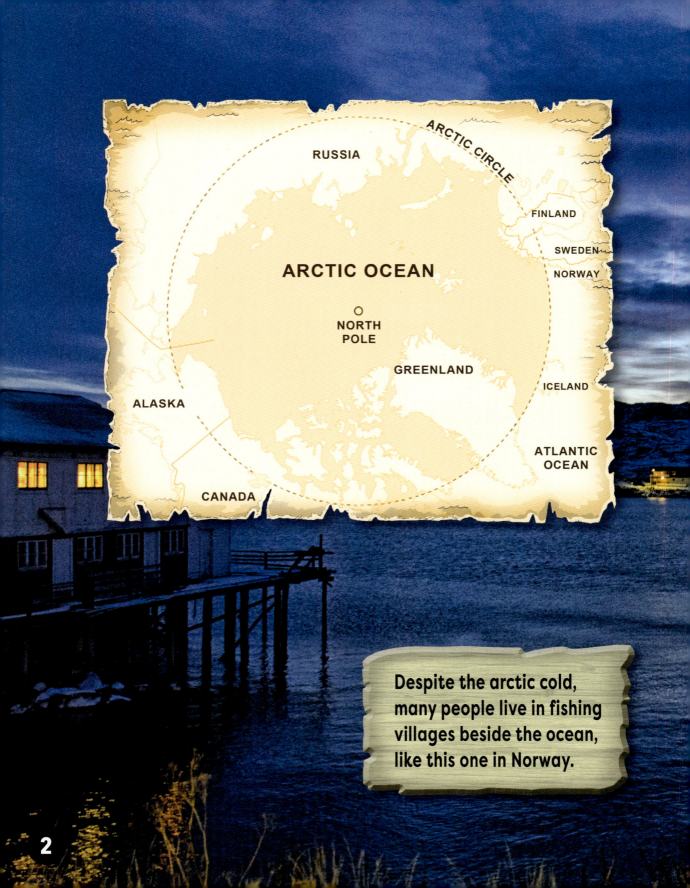

Despite the arctic cold, many people live in fishing villages beside the ocean, like this one in Norway.

If you want to visit the Arctic Ocean, make sure you pack your warmest clothes. It surrounds the North Pole, so it's very cold! Even though it is the smallest ocean in the world, it still covers about 5.4 million square miles (14 million square kilometers). That is almost one and a half times bigger than the entire United States.

Many animals in the Arctic Ocean eat plankton, tiny plants and animals that drift along in the ocean currents. This type is called krill. They only grow to about 2 inches (5.1 centimeters) in size.

The Arctic Ocean is landlocked. This means it is surrounded on every side by land. The deepest spot in this ocean is the Eurasian Basin (yur-AY-zhun BAY-sin). It is 17,880 feet (5,449.8 meters) deep, which means you could stack almost 1,000 adult male giraffes in it!

The Arctic Ocean has the least amount of salt of all the oceans. It is also incredibly cold. In the summer, the water will only reach about 32 degrees Fahrenheit (0 degrees Celsius). During the winter, it is often *way* below zero degrees Fahrenheit (-18 degrees Celsius)! The animals that live here have adapted to this extreme cold.

One of the most common fish in the Arctic Ocean is the polar cod. They have an antifreeze protein in their blood that keeps them from freezing in the cold Arctic waters.

Polar bears are the largest bears on earth. Standing up, they can reach up to 12 feet (3.7 meters) tall! All the wild polar bears in the world are found in the Arctic region. They spend more time in the water or on sea ice than they do on land. Their white coats help them hide to better catch their prey.

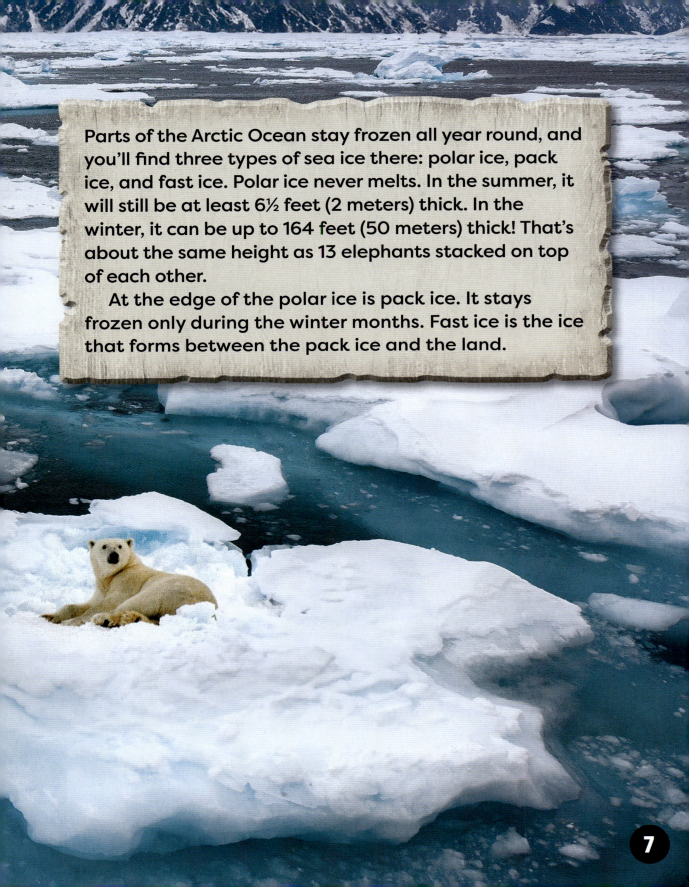

Parts of the Arctic Ocean stay frozen all year round, and you'll find three types of sea ice there: polar ice, pack ice, and fast ice. Polar ice never melts. In the summer, it will still be at least 6½ feet (2 meters) thick. In the winter, it can be up to 164 feet (50 meters) thick! That's about the same height as 13 elephants stacked on top of each other.

At the edge of the polar ice is pack ice. It stays frozen only during the winter months. Fast ice is the ice that forms between the pack ice and the land.

Bowhead whales are considered to be the longest-living mammal on earth. They can live over 200 years. The "bow" or hump shape of its head helps it break through the ice.

A number of whales swim in the incredibly cold Arctic Ocean waters. The bowhead whale can grow up to 60 feet (18.3 meters) long and weigh up to 100 US tons (90.7 metric tons). This is about the same as fifteen elephants! The bowhead has the largest mouth of any animal on earth. The baleen plates it uses to filter food from the water can grow up to 13 feet (4 meters) long. It swims along the ocean floor with its mouth open, scooping up large quantities of plankton to eat.

One of the best known Arctic whales is the beluga whale. They are the only whales that are normally white. Their color helps them hide from polar bears and killer whales. The round bump on a beluga's head is an organ for echolocation called a "melon." They are known as "the canary of the seas" because of their high-pitched calls.

Beluga whales can easily swim just below the ice because they don't have dorsal fins (fins on their backs).

Many of the world's icebergs and glaciers are found in the Arctic Ocean. Glaciers **(GLEY-shers)** are large sheets of ice. They can spread out over miles. Icebergs are large pieces of glaciers that have broken off. They move through the water, pushed by water currents. Icebergs smaller than 16 feet (4.9 meters) across are often called "growlers." The undersides of icebergs and sea ice are home to thousands of different algae species. The algae is an important ocean food source.

Glaciers contain about 69 percent of all the fresh water in the world. If they all melted at once, sea levels would rise about 230 feet (70.1 meters).

Arctic terns dive under the water at high speeds to chase and catch fish to eat.

Arctic terns migrate long distances, traveling as far as the coast of Antarctica. They always nest in the summer on land near the Arctic Ocean. While the females are nesting, the male terns dive for fish to provide food.

Little auks mate for life and always lay a single egg when they nest. They often use the same nest site every year.

Little auks live in large colonies on islands around the Arctic Ocean and other cold waters. They swim underwater near ice edges and coastlines to find their food. They really are "little," only growing to about 8¼ inches (21 centimeters) tall and weighing around 7 ounces (198.4 grams) at most.

The narwhal (NAR-wall) is a whale that is known for its tusk, a long tooth that grows from its upper lip. This tooth senses any changes in water temperature and can grow up to 10 feet (3 meters) long. It has earned the whale the nickname "unicorn of the sea." The narwhal can live up to 100 years and uses echolocation to find its prey.

Because there is less sea ice in the Arctic Ocean every year, killer whales are spending much more time there. Killer whales prey on narwhals, so this change has disrupted many narwhal behaviors and habitats.

The narwhal is able to communicate by squealing, trilling, and clicking. The males sometimes use their tusks as a weapon when fighting with other males.

Walruses (WALL-russ-es) are huge marine mammals. Some grow as long as 11 feet (3.4 meters) and weigh up to 3,700 pounds (1,678.3 kilograms). They have flippers, a wide head, small eyes, tusks, and whiskers. They use their tusks to cut through ice, in self-defense, and to help pull themselves up out of the water. They spend two-thirds of their lives on the sea ice.

Walruses have 400 to 700 whiskers. They use these sensitive whiskers to find buried food like clams and mussels.

Sea spiders are not really spiders, even though they look a lot like them. They have tiny bodies and walk on the tips of their long, thin legs.

The bottom of the Arctic Ocean is extremely cold and dark, but the seafloor is still filled with life. Animals known as "benthos," like brittle stars, snails, sea spiders, and crabs, eat the algae and other materials that sink down from the ice above.

Snow crabs live an average of 14 to 16 years. They grow in size by "molting," shedding their old shell and growing another. Male crab shells, known as carapaces, can grow up to 6½ inches (16.5 centimeters) in diameter.

The Arctic Ocean has large areas covered by sea ice, which forms and melts entirely in the ocean. Far beneath the ice, you'll find creatures like the Greenland shark, the only shark that can live in the Arctic Ocean year-round.

The Greenland shark is the longest-living vertebrate (animal with a spine) in the world. We've found some that were 400 years old, and scientists think they could live up to 500 years.

Harp seals are expert swimmers and divers, who hunt for fish deep in the ocean. They can stay under the water for up to 15 minutes at a time and can dive up to 1,300 feet (396.2 meters) deep. That's at least 25 times deeper than human adults can dive! Their blubber helps to keep them warm, and their bodies are perfect for handling the high pressure of deep, cold water.

Baby harp seals are famous for their snowy white fur, which helps to absorb sunlight and keep them warm until their bodies develop blubber. They shed the fur when they are three to four weeks old to become silver-gray.

The ringed seal is the most common seal in the Arctic Ocean. They live an average of 40 years, and their whole lives revolve around the sea ice. They are among the smallest seals in the world, weighing only around 110 to 150 pounds (50 to 68 kilograms).

As temperatures rise because of global warming, the ice in the Arctic melts faster and the sea levels rise. Animals like the ringed seal, which depend on the ice, struggle to survive.

FURTHER READING

Books

Gonzales, Doreen. *The Frigid Arctic Ocean.* Berkeley Heights, NJ: Enslow Elementary, 2013.

Green, Jen. *Arctic Ocean.* New York: Gareth Stevens Publishing, 2006.

Isaacs, Sally. *Helen Thayer's Arctic Adventure: A Woman and a Dog Walk to the North Pole.* Mankato, MN: Capstone Young Readers, 2016.

Oachs, Emily Rose. *Arctic Ocean.* Minneapolis, MN: Bellwether Media, 2016.

Spilsbury, Louise, and Richard Spilsbury. *Arctic Ocean.* Portsmouth, NH: Heinemann, 2015.

Woods, Michael. *Seven Natural Wonders of the Arctic, Antarctica, and the Oceans.* Minneapolis, MN: Twenty-First Century Books, 2009.

Web Sites

Defenders of Wildlife: "Arctic"
https://defenders.org/wild-places/arctic

iTV.com: "Top 10 Facts You Need to Know about the Arctic"
https://www.itv.com/news/2013-04-10/top-10-facts-you-need-to-know-about-the-arctic

National Geographic Kids: "10 Facts about the Arctic!"
https://www.natgeokids.com/uk/discover/geography/general-geography/ten-facts-about-the-arctic/

GLOSSARY

basin (BAY-sin)—A natural bowl-shaped space that holds water.

current (KUR-rent)—An area of water that moves in one direction.

echolocation (EK-oh-loh-KAY-shun)—Finding objects by sending out sounds and determining the time it takes for the echo to return.

glacier (GLAY-shur)—A huge, moving mass of ice formed from snow.

global warming (GLOW-bull WAR-ming)—The increase in earth's average temperatures causing changes in climate.

iceberg (Ahys burg)—A large, floating mass of ice broken off of a glacier.

landlocked (Land-lokd)—Shut in completely or almost completely by land.

narwhal (NAR-wall)—A type of whale that is known for the long tusk that grows from its upper lip.

plankton (PLANK-ton)—Tiny organisms that drift in water. Plankton is a major food source for many different animals.

prey (PRAY)—An animal hunted for food.

tusk (TUSK)—An extremely long tooth found in creatures such as elephants and walruses.

walruses (WALL-russ-es)—Huge marine mammals that have wide heads, small eyes, whiskers, and two large, downward-pointing tusks.

PHOTO CREDITS

pp. 2-4, 14 (inset)—Christopher Michel; pp. 6-7—Shutterstock/Steve Allen; p. 8 (inset)—Shutterstock/Wildnerdpix; p. 10 (inset)—Shutterstock/Marco De Luca; pp. 10-11—Shutterstock/Jakob Rippe; pp. 12-13—Shutterstock/Mozgova; p. 13 (inset)—Alan Schmierer; pp.14-15—Shutterstock/Byron Layton; p. 15 (inset)—Shutterstock/Apolla; pp. 16-17—Shutterstock/Agami Photo Agency; p. 19 (inset)—Shutterstock/boybehindacamera; pp. 20-21—AWeith; pp. 22-23—Shutterstock/Kondratuk Aleksei; pp. 24-25—Shutterstock/Dotted Yeti; p. 25 (inset)—Hemming1952; pp. 26-27—Shutterstock/ slowmotiongli; p. 26 (inset)—Shutterstock/Dolores M. Harvey; pp. 28-29—Shutterstock/Robert Harding Video; p. 29 (inset)— Shutterstock/Sergey Uryadnikov. All other photos—Public Domain.

INDEX

Algae 12, 22
Arctic Ocean
   glaciers 12–13
   global warming 29
   ice 6, 7, 9, 10, 12, 17, 19, 20, 22, 24, 28, 29
   temperature 4, 18, 29
Arctic terns 14–15
Eurasian Basin 4
Greenland sharks 24–25
Harp seals 26–27
Icebergs 12
Little auks 16–17
Ocean currents 4
Orca (killer whale) 10, 19
Plankton 4, 9
Polar cod 5
Polar bears 1, 6–7, 10
Ringed seals 28–29
Sea spider 22
Snow crab 22–23
Walrus 20–21
Whales
   Beluga 10–11
   Bowhead 8–9
   Narwhal 18–19
   Orca (killer whale) 10, 19

© 2025 by Curious Fox Books™, an imprint of Fox Chapel Publishing Company, Inc.

Amazing Creatures of the Arctic Ocean is a revision of *Water Planet: Life in the Arctic Ocean*, originally published in 2018 by Purple Toad Publishing, Inc. Reproduction of its contents is strictly prohibited without written permission from the rights holder.

Paperback ISBN 979-8-89094-172-5
Hardcover ISBN 979-8-89094-173-2

Library of Congress Control Number: 2024949950

To learn more about the other great books from Fox Chapel Publishing, or to find a retailer near you, call toll-free at 800-457-9112 or visit us at *www.FoxChapelPublishing.com*.
You can also send mail to:
Fox Chapel Publishing
903 Square Street
Mount Joy, PA 17552

We are always looking for talented authors. To submit an idea, please send a brief inquiry to acquisitions@foxchapelpublishing.com.

Fox Chapel Publishing makes every effort to use environmentally friendly paper for printing.

Printed in China